Come to My House

Children's Poetry

Edited by
Patricia Almada and Teresa Lo-Cascio

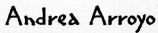

Illustrated by
Andrea Arroyo

Rigby

The six children who wrote the poems
in this book are all bilingual speakers
of Spanish and English. They attend
New River Elementary School in Norwalk,
California.

© 1999 by Rigby,
a division of Reed Elsevier Inc.
1000 Hart Rd.
Barrington, IL 60010-2627

Executive Editor: Lynelle H. Morgenthaler
Design assistance provided by Lindaanne Donohoe Design

04 03
10 9 8 7 6

Printed in Singapore

ISBN 0-7635-5703-X

Every family has things they like to do and things they like to eat—things that stay the same year after year. These are family traditions.

This collection of poetry is about family traditions. Jesse, Sonia, Nancy, Cecy, Xotchilt, and Jonathan share their feelings about a family tradition that has special meaning for them.

Come to My House

Jesse García

Another year has gone by.
At my house, the family arrives.
The sweet aroma of tamales and pozole
fills every room like New Year's Eve perfume.
In the garage the stereo blares—we dance.

You should come to my house on New Year's Eve.
The ceilings of all the rooms
are covered with balloons,
colorful candy clouds to pop at midnight.
In the garage the stereo blares—we hug.

You should come to my house on New Year's Eve.
We eat one grape for each month of the year,
twelve months, twelve grapes,
one wish for the months to come.
In the garage the stereo blares—we eat.

You should come to my house on New Year's Eve.
We dance, eat, and enjoy each other's company.
The last of the year slowly creeps by.
The whole family spends the night.
In the garage the stereo gets turned off—
    we sleep.

Braids

Sonia Gutiérrez

All the girls in my family wear braids.
There are big, bulky braids
    and slim, slender braids.
There are long, lanky braids
    and short, shiny braids.
I always wear a single braid
    snaking slowly down my back.
I hate it when my hair isn't braided,
    it gets twisted like spaghetti on a fork.
Then my Mom brushes it gently,
    untangling each and every knot.
Like a black waterfall or a smooth, silky cloth,
    my hair is ready for braiding once more.

Pupusas

Nancy Quintanilla

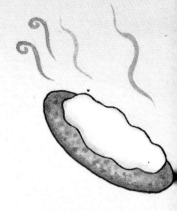

Pupusas are round, soft, and tasty

Usually grilled in a pan

Puffy treats with sour cream topping

Unique from all other foods

So good they make me smile

All day long

Special because they remind me of El Salvador

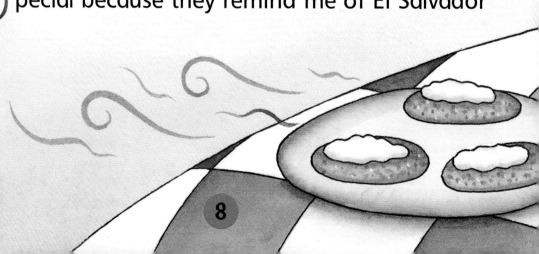

Family Time

Cecy Baños

Bang . . . bang . . . bang . . .
   open the cabinets,
   reach for the things we need.

Whistle . . . whistle . . . whistle . . .
   blows the kettle,
   telling us the water for coffee is ready.

Glug . . . glug . . . glug . . .
   pour milk into the mugs
   for the children in the family.

Clank . . . clank . . . clank . . .
   carry mugs and plates,
   balancing everything on a tray.

Plop . . . plop . . . plop . . .
   dip minloga into our cups,
   a crunchy, sweet-filled bread.

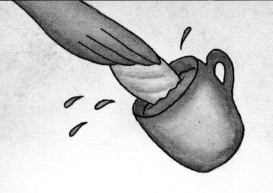

Buzz . . . buzz . . . buzz . . .
  talk about our day
  and my brother's soccer game.

Ha . . . ha . . . ha . . .
  enjoy each other's company,
  sharing time together.

Zzz . . . zzz . . . zzz . . .
  doze off on my mother's lap,
  sleepy like a kitten after a bowl of milk.

Rice, Rice, and More Rice

Xotchilt Alcántar

Rice with fish,
rice with chicken,
rice with meat,
rice is always a special treat!

It's rice, rice, and more rice.
Every day we eat rice.

In the Dominican Republic,
my parents grew up eating rice.
They ate rice morning, noon, and night.
Now rice is our American delight.

It's rice, rice, and more rice.
Every day we eat rice.

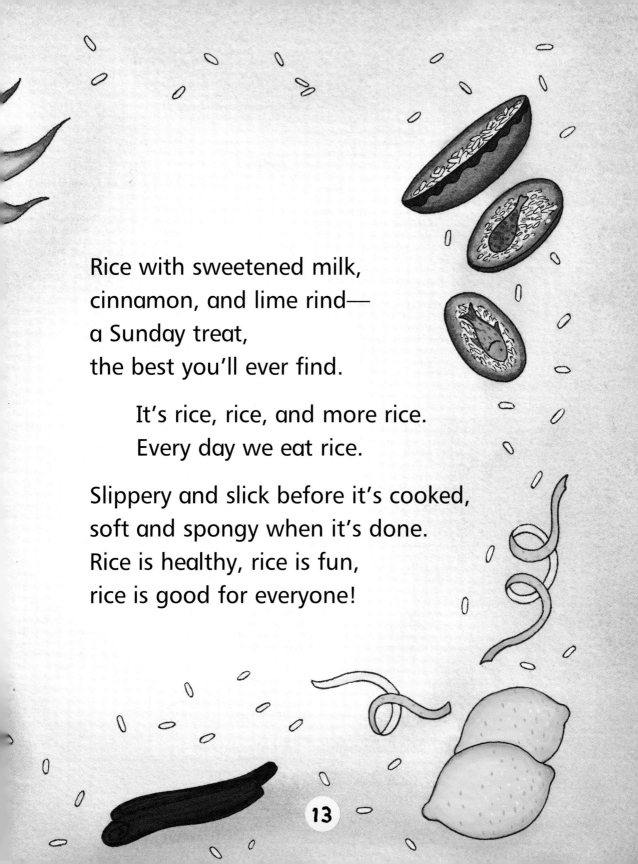

Rice with sweetened milk,
cinnamon, and lime rind—
a Sunday treat,
the best you'll ever find.

It's rice, rice, and more rice.
Every day we eat rice.

Slippery and slick before it's cooked,
soft and spongy when it's done.
Rice is healthy, rice is fun,
rice is good for everyone!

Story Time

Jonathan Ruiz

I remember when I was little,
story time was fun, so much fun.
I brushed my teeth and jumped in bed,
then reached for Shamu, my best friend.

I was tucked in very tight
and waited patiently
until Mommy or Daddy
came in for story time.

Daddy sat on a chair
at the side of my bed.
Mommy lay next to me
and brought my teddy bear.

Settled down in my bed,
calm as a sailboat on a lake,
I shut my eyelids slowly,
pictures fluttering in my head.

Then a gentle hug and a kiss on the cheek,
the lights went out and I was all alone.
The pictures became blurry and before long
I was ready for a good night's sleep.

Meet the Poets

Jesse García

third grade

Jesse likes singing and dancing and wants to be an artist. He enjoys the work of Claude Monet and the music of the Mexican group Los Tucanes. His parents are from Mexico.

Nancy Quintanilla

fifth grade

Nancy wants to go to the University of California–Los Angeles. She hopes to become an elementary school teacher. Her mom and dad are from El Salvador.

Xotchilt Alcántar

fifth grade

Xotchilt enjoys spending time with her family. She loves to read and write! Xotchilt is proud of her Dominican and Cuban heritage.

Sonia Gutiérrez

fourth grade

Sonia wants to be a teacher. She enjoys reading chapter books in her spare time. Sonia's parents are from Mexico.

Cecy Baños

fifth grade

Cecy wants to go to Harvard and graduate with a law degree. She knows how to talk people into doing things! Her parents are from El Salvador.

Jonathan Ruiz

fourth grade

Jonathan is a gifted artist who loves to draw and make paper sculptures. He enjoys the art of Vincent Van Gogh, especially *The Starry Night*. His parents are from Mexico.